Short Vowels

Joyce Dadouche, M.A.
Laura L. Rogan, Ph.D.
Janis Wennberg, M.A.

Cove Foundation, Winnetka, Illinois

SRA/McGraw-Hill
Columbus, Ohio

ISBN 0-02-686972-1

3 4 5 6 7 8 9 10 MAL 99 98 97 96

Contents

A_
a_

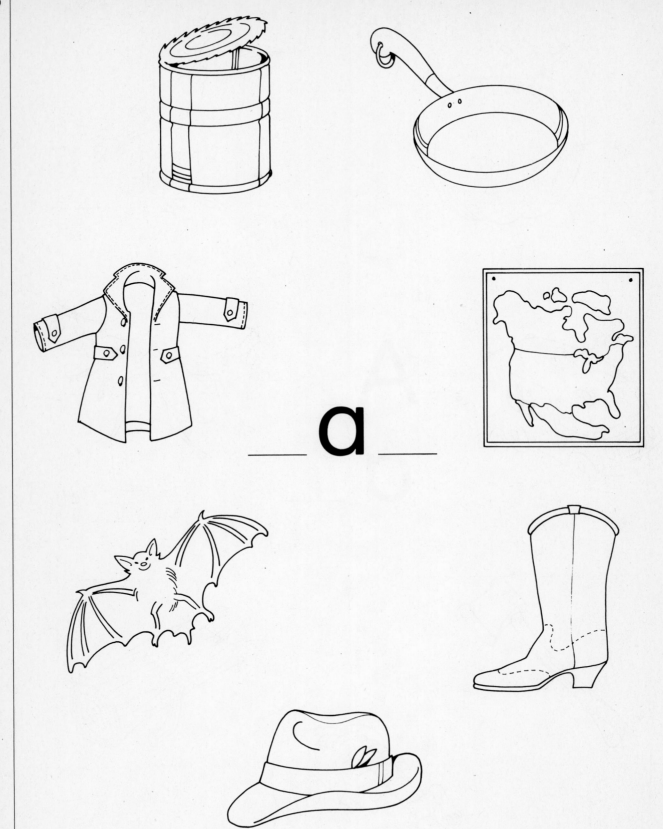

a

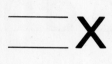 

_ _ x  c _ n

 c _ t    m _ n

 _ _ x    c _ n

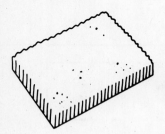 m _ t    p _ n

a a a a a a a a a

a families

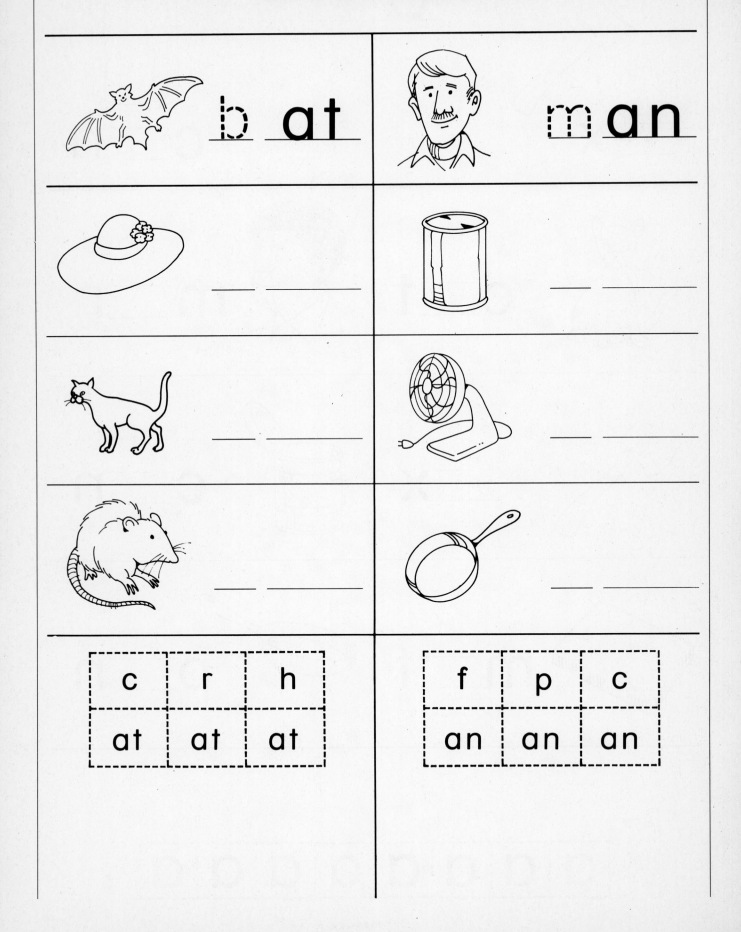

a families

a families

a families

 d **ad**   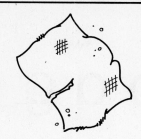 r **ag**

 _____   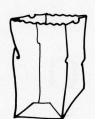 _____

 _____   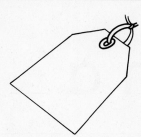 _____

 _____    _____

s	m	p
ad	ad	ad

t	b	w
ag	ag	ag

a

 b a g

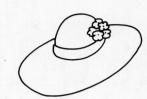 h a __

 f a __

 f a __

 h a __

 w a __

 m a __

 t a __

| g | g | m | n | p | t | t |

a_

 j a _

 r a _

 _ a t

 _ a d

 _ a _

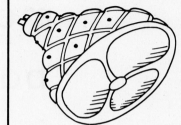 _ a _

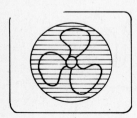 _ a _

 _ a _

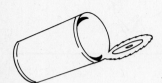 _ a _

 _ a _

b	c	c	d	f	g	h	h
m	m	n	n	n	t	t	v

a

b__t   v__n   m__d   s__d

w__g   j__m   b__g   m__p

mad

bat

map

bag

sád

wag

jam

van

pan	pan	fan	pop	an	pan
jam	jot	sam	jam	jam	jet
mat	mat	man	mat	map	nap
cap	cat	cap	can	cop	cap
fan	fan	tan	fan	fed	an

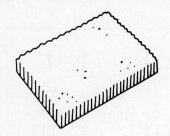 mat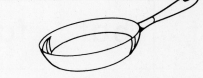

 fan

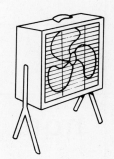 cap

pan

map

fat

can

cat

fat	bat	fat	rat	cat	fat
can	an	can	fan	cat	can
cat	sat	cat	at	cat	can
ham	ham	had	hat	ham	tam
map	man	map	sap	map	nap

a___

cab	bat	ax
ham	mad	wag
nap	rat	van

cab cap nap	sag has sad
man mat can	jam jab fan
tag bat bag	map nap pan
tag rag tap	ban bad bat

a _

Pat has a __ __ __.

Dad has a __ __ __.

Pam has a __ __ __.

The man has a __ __ __.

Dad has the __ __ __.

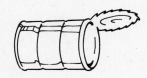
Nan has the __ __ __.

| cap | jam | hat | can | fan | bat |

Sam has a __ __ __.

The man has a __ __ __.

Pam can pat the __ __ __.

Jan __ __ __ the __ __ __.

Dan __ __ __ a tan __ __ __.

The __ __ __ has a __ __ __.

has	man	has	nap	cap
can	cat	hat	bat	can

1.

__ __ __ __ __ __ __ __ .

2.

__ __ __ __ __ __ __ __ .

3.

__ __ __ __ __ __ __ __ .

1.	bat	a	has	Dad	
2.	pan	has	Jan	the	
3.	cat	A	a	nap	has

_ O _

O

_ _ x

p _ p

p _ t

c _ t

b _ x

_ _ x

_ n

p _ p

o o o o o o o o

o families

p **op**

c **ot**

t	m	h
op	op	op

p	d	h
ot	ot	ot

o families

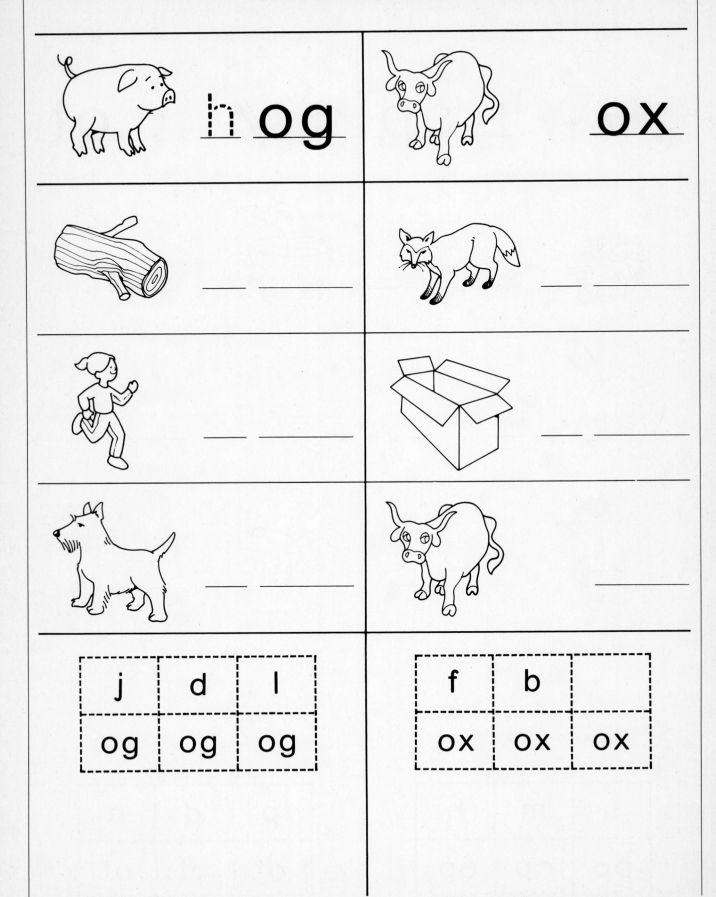

h **og**   **ox**

j | d | l
og | og | og

f | b
ox | ox | ox

O_

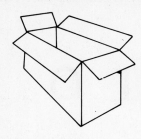 b o _    m o _

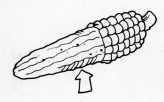 c o _    f o _

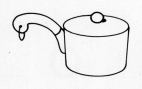 p o _   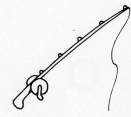 r o _

 h o _    h o _

 o _    l o _

b	d	g	g	p	p	t	x	x	x

O

p o _

r o _

_ o p

_ o g

_ o _

_ o _

_ o _

_ o _

_ o _

_ o _

b	d	d	f	g	g	j	l
m	p	p	p	t	t	x	x

O

m□p   □n   p□t   t□p

p□p   f□x   h□p   c□t

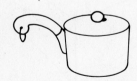

top

pot

hop

cot

on

mop

fox

pop

O

hop	hat	hop	pop	top	hop
dot	dot	tot	tod	dot	top
pot	pot	top	pot	pan	cot
mop	mom	mop	mop	top	hop
box	fox	bun	box	ox	box

box

pot

hop

mop

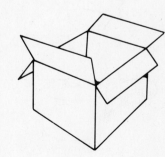

O

top

fox

pop

cot

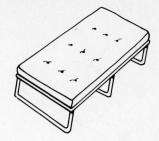

fox	fox	fun	box	mop	fox
cot	not	cot	cat	not	cot
pop	pod	cop	top	pop	pop
top	tap	top	cot	top	pot
hot	hot	hop	pot	hat	hot

O

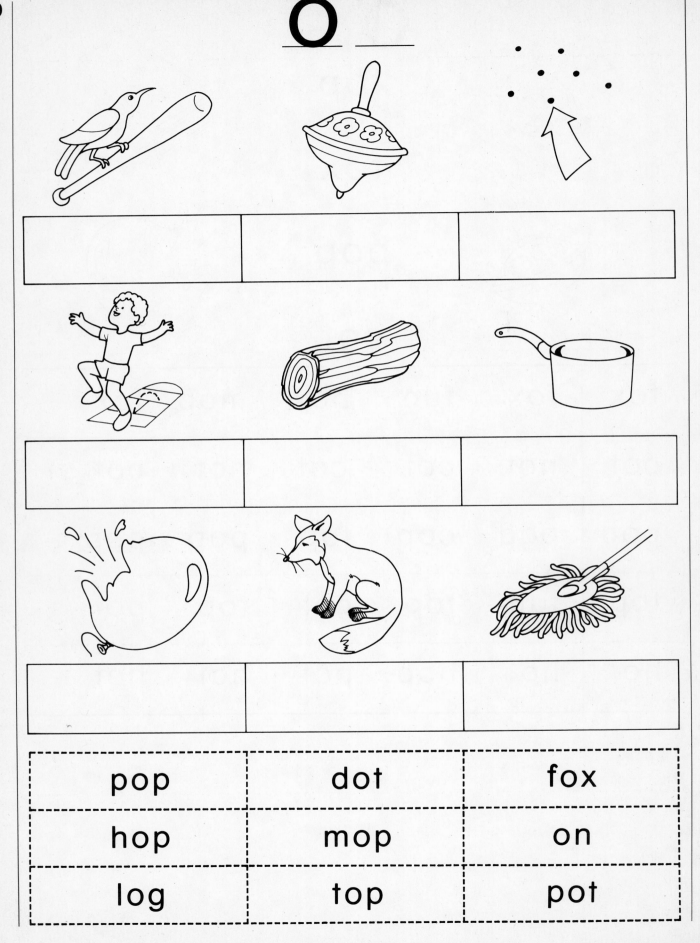

pop	dot	fox
hop	mop	on
log	top	pot

O

fox box ox	log lot tot
pot top pop	top pot got
on hot hop	top tot hot
on mom not	dot on dog
top tot dot	fog ox fox

O_

 a fox on a __ __ __

 a rod on the __ __ __

 a mop on a __ __ __

 hop on a __ __ __

 a dot on a __ __ __

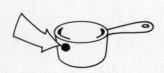 a dog on a __ __ __

| log | box | pop | top | pot | cot |

a fox ___ a box

a top __ __ the ___ ___ ___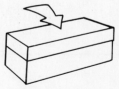

a ___ ___ ___ on the ___ ___ ___

a dog on a ___ ___ ___

a ___ ___ ___ __ __ __ the cot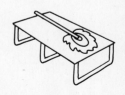

box	box	top	log	mop
on	on	on	on	on

1.

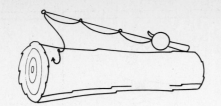

_ _

2.

_ _

3.

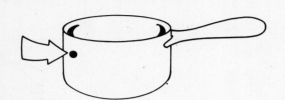

_ _

1.				
rod	a	on	the	log
2. pot	dot	on	the	a
3. a	the	box	on	top

a	o			

m _ p   c _ p   h _ t   p _ t

f _ t   c _ t   r _ d   t _ p

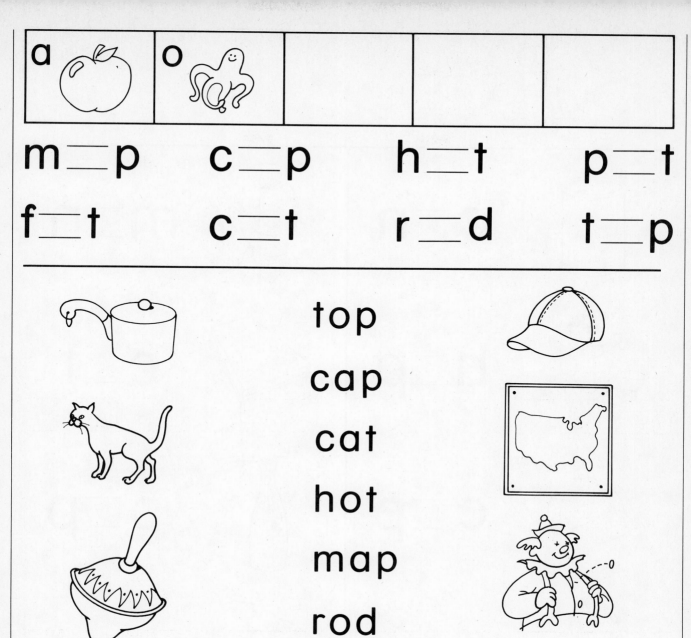

top

cap

cat

hot

map

rod

pot

fat

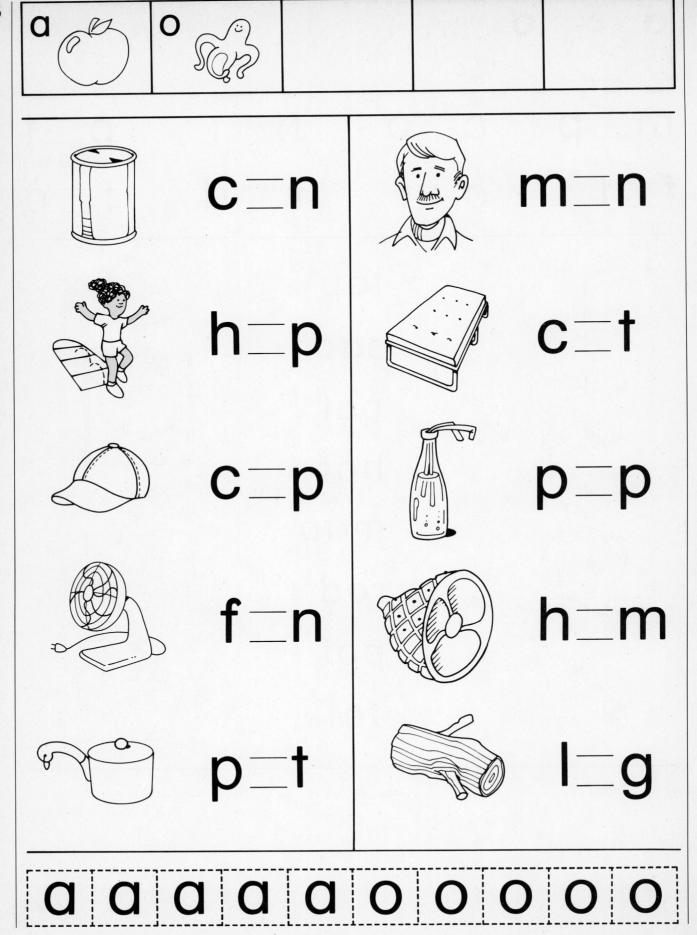

| a | o | | | |

c _ n   m _ n

h _ p   c _ t

c _ p   p _ p

f _ n   h _ m

p _ t   l _ g

a a a a a o o o o o

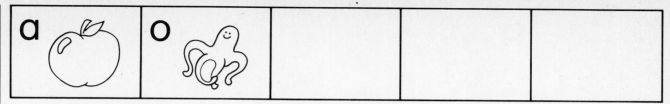

| a | o | | | |

---

mom on not	mop mat man	hot log lot
sag gap gas	ham hot hat	hat hot hop
dot dog log	ox fox box	pan pop pot
ox ax box	cot cab cat	mop map mat

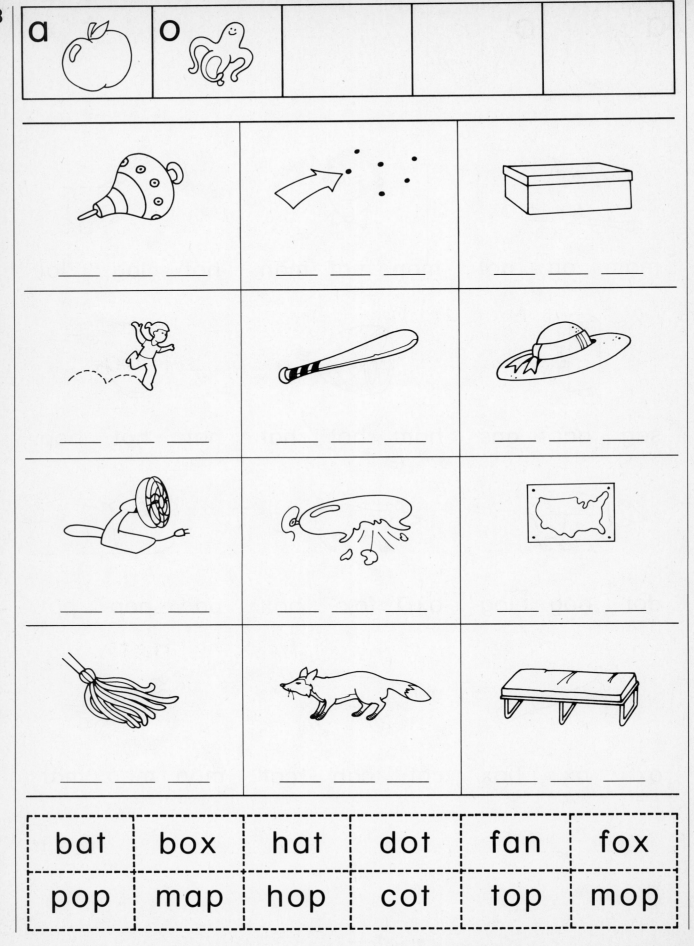

| a | o | | | |

bat | box | hat | dot | fan | fox
pop | map | hop | cot | top | mop

| a | o | | | |

1. The man has a _____.

rat rod nod

2. A cat has a _____.

nap not had

3. Mom has a _____.

pat pot got

4. Pam has a _____.

had hot hat

5. The cab has _____.

gas got pan

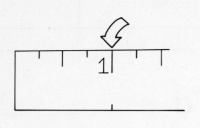

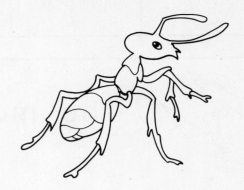

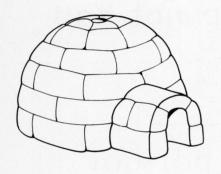

I ___

i ___

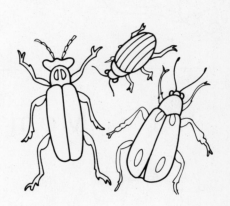

_ i _

i

__n

p__n

h__t

d__g

__n

k__t

w__g

p__n

i i i i i i i i

i families

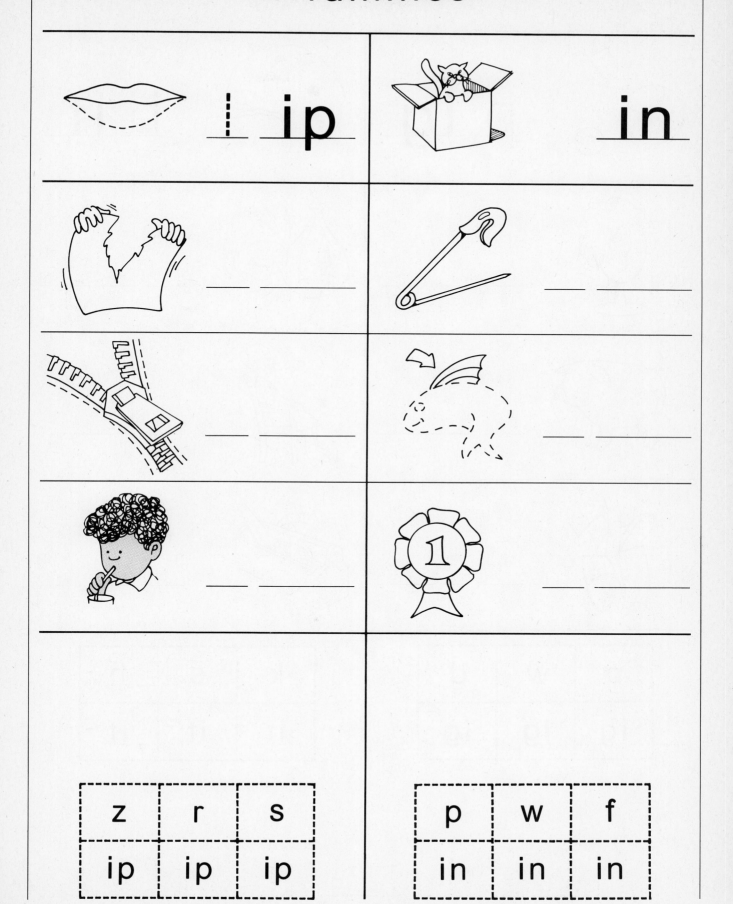

	ip		in
(lips)		(cat in box)	
(rip)	____	(pin)	____
(zip)	____	(fin)	____
(sip)	____	(win)	____

z	r	s
ip	ip	ip

p	w	f
in	in	in

i families

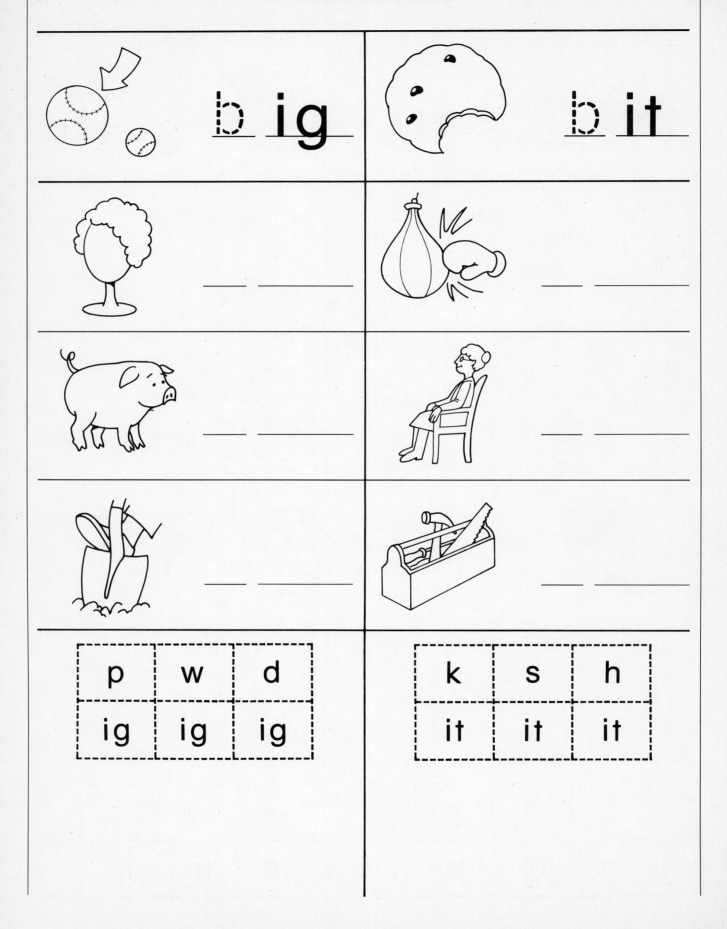

b __ig__

b __it__

i

 w i _

 f i _

 p i _

 i _

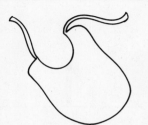 b i _

 d i _

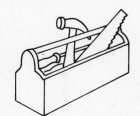 k i _

 l i _

 l i _

 p i _

b	d	g	g	g	n	n	n	p	t

 p i _

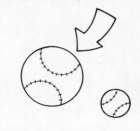 b i _

 _ i n

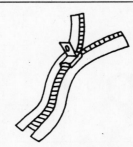 _ i p

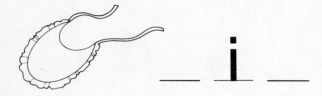 _ i _

 _ i _

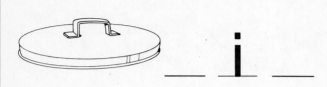 _ i _

 _ i _

 _ i _

 _ i _

b	b	d	d	f	g	g	g
h	l	l	p	s	t	x	z

i

d __ g   b __ b   s __ x   p __ n

w __ g   l __ p   s __ t   l __ d

pin

six

bib

lid

lip

wig

dig

sit

i

rip	rid	rip	rig	rip	nip
fix	mix	fin	fix	fin	fix
bib	bib	dip	bib	tip	bit
six	mix	six	sin	six	mix
fin	him	fix	fin	fix	fin

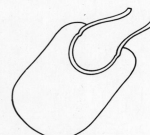

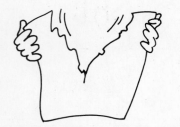

fin

bib

rip

six

i

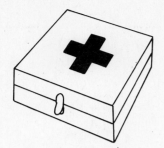

hit

kit

sit

lip

kit	hit	fit	kit	hid	kit
sit	sip	sit	sin	hit	sit
lid	lid	lip	lid	lit	hit
hit	him	hip	hit	hit	hid
lip	lit	lip	lid	lip	lit

i

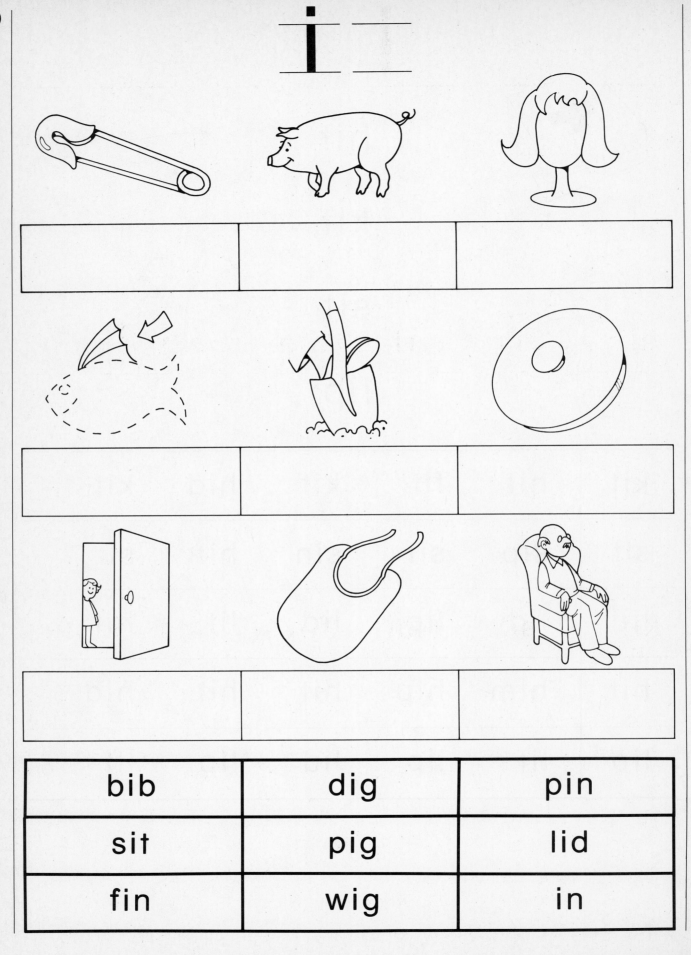

bib	dig	pin
sit	pig	lid
fin	wig	in

pin	in	pig	pit	pin	pig
nip	rib	rip	dig	pig	dip
dig	lid	lip	it	in	pin
kit	sit	bit	fin	him	tin
sip	hit	sit	pig	wig	wit

It is a ___ ___ ___ .

A pin is in the ___ ___ ___ .

The bib did ___ ___ ___ .

It is a big ___ ___ ___ .

Kim is ___ ___ ___ .

Did Tim ___ ___ ___ ?

| kit | six | win | pig | wig | rip |

A pin is __ __ the kit.

Jim __ __ __ his lip.

__ __ is a __ __ __ pig.

Tim __ __ __ win the __ __ __ .

Kim did __ __ __ the __ __ __ .

big	did	bit	pin	lid
It	is	fix	in	rip

1.

__ __ __ __

2.

__ __ __ __ __ .

3.

__ __ __ __ __ .

1. rip	a	a	in	bib
2. did	fix	it	Tim	
3. pin	Kim	the	hid	

| a 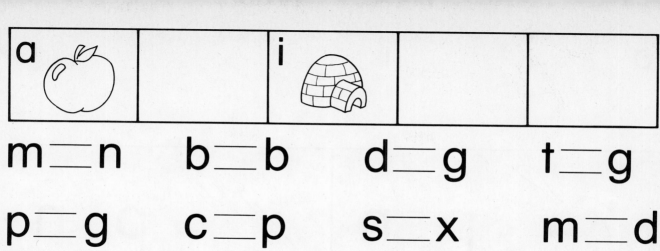 | | i | | |

m⬚n b⬚b d⬚g t⬚g

p⬚g c⬚p s⬚x m⬚d

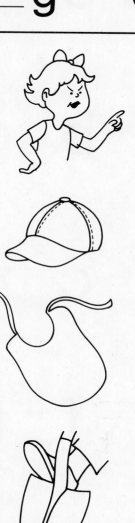

bib

six

mad

tag

dig

pig

cap

man

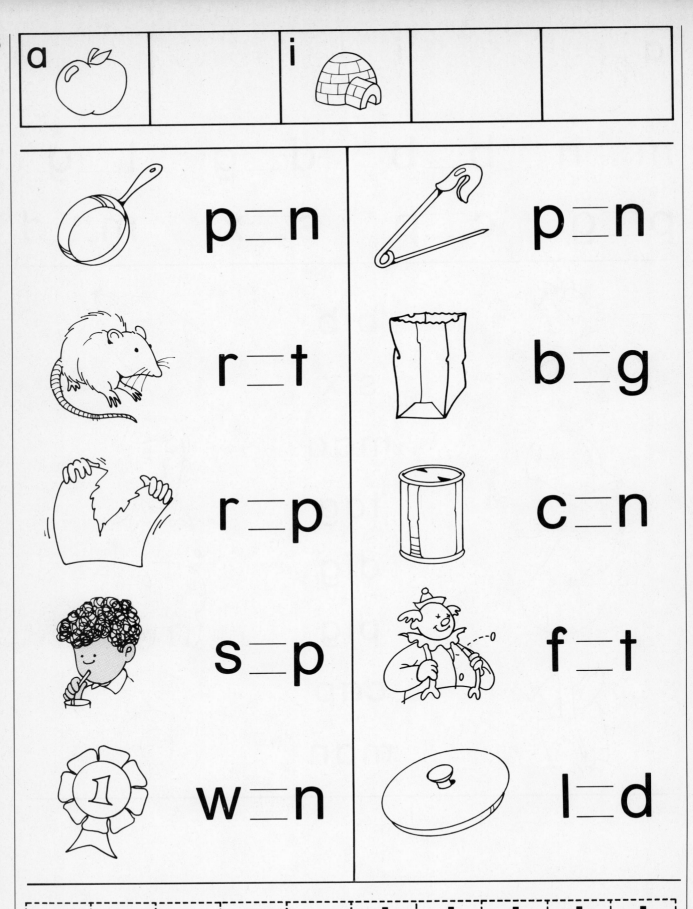

| a | | i | | |

p _ n

p _ n

r _ t

b _ g

r _ p

c _ n

s _ p

f _ t

w _ n

l _ d

a a a a a i i i i i

---

a    **i**

57

cat   cab   kit

fat   fan   fin

hid   had   hit

wig   wag   rat

sip   sap   sit

big   bag   bit

ham   hat   hit

fit   fun   fin

wig   wag   rat

pin   pan   pat

nip   nap   map

ham   him   hat

© 1995 SRA/McGraw-Hill

58

| a 🍎 | | i ⛺ | | |

_ _ _	_ _ _	_ _ _
_ _ _	_ _ _	_ _ _
_ _ _	_ _ _	_ _ _
_ _ _	_ _ _	_ _ _

| mat | lid | map | lip | win | big |
| sad | rip | mad | van | man | bib |

a	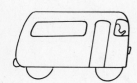		i		

1.

Jim has a _____.

bat bit big

2.

Kim can _____.

hat hit has

3.

A man has a _____.

ham hat hit

4.

The van is _____.

bit bag big

5.

Pam has a _____.

bag big tap

| a  | o | i | | |

l ☐ d   s ☐ d   p ☐ g   p ☐ n

h ☐ p   m ☐ d   b ☐ x   d ☐ t

pig

pin

dot

box

mad

hop

lid

sad

a	o	i		

 _n

 f_n

 w_g

 c_t

 l_g

 f_n

 p_n

 _n

 w_g

 d_g

a	a	a	o	o	o	i	i	i	i

| **a** | o 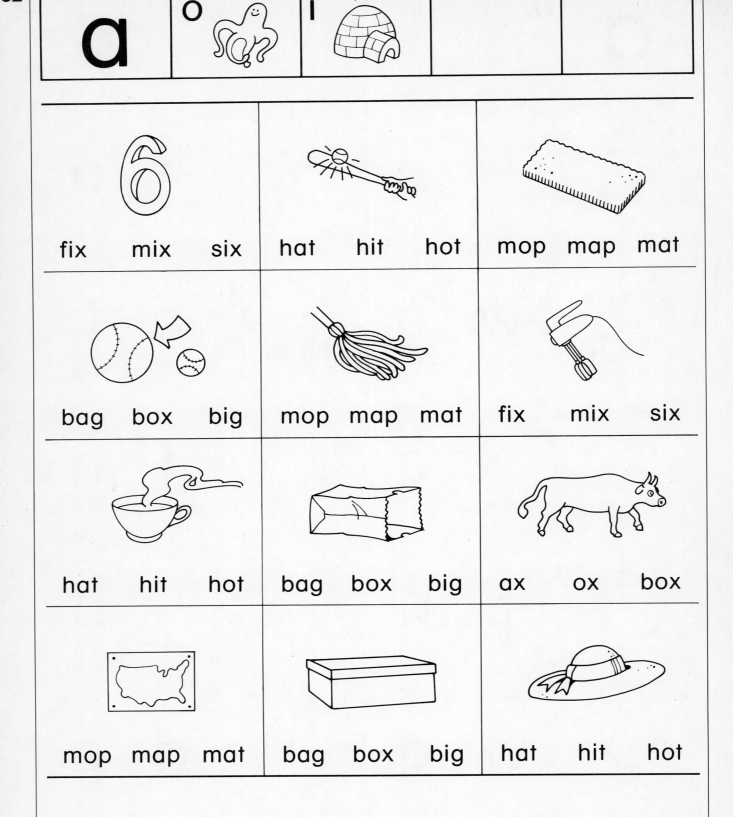 | i | | |

fix   mix   six

hat   hit   hot

mop   map   mat

bag   box   big

mop   map   mat

fix   mix   six

hat   hit   hot

bag   box   big

ax   ox   box

mop   map   mat

bag   box   big

hat   hit   hot

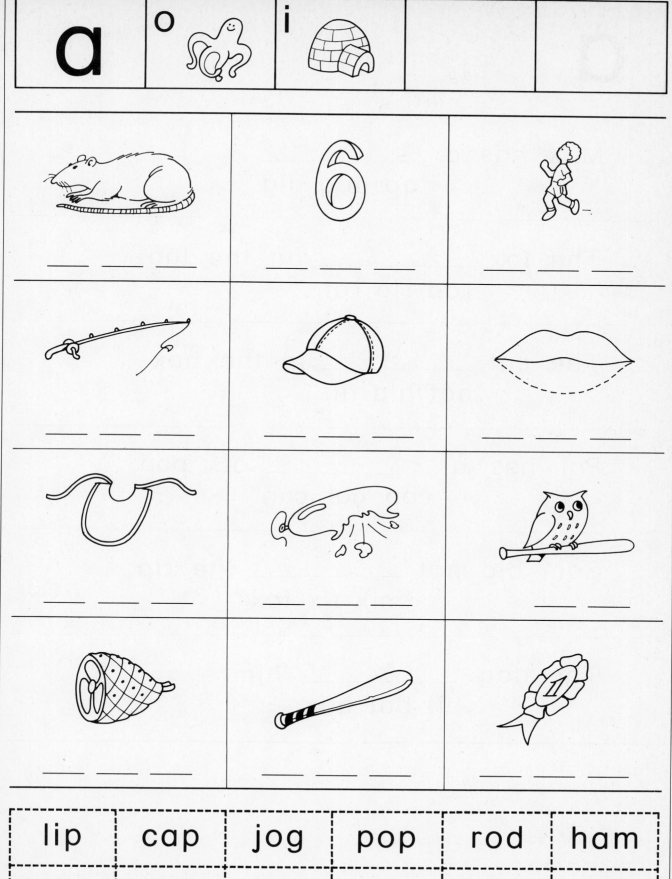

| a | o | i | | |

| lip | cap | jog | pop | rod | ham |
| win | bat | bib | on | six | rat |

a	o	i 		

1.

Max has a _____.

tap dog dig

2.

The fox _____ on the log.

rod rip ran

3.

The cat _____ in the box.

hat hid hit

4.

Pat has a _____ of pop.

cap cot can

5.

Sam did not _____ the rip.

mix fix fox

6.

The dog _____ him.

bit bat box

U__

u__

u

u __

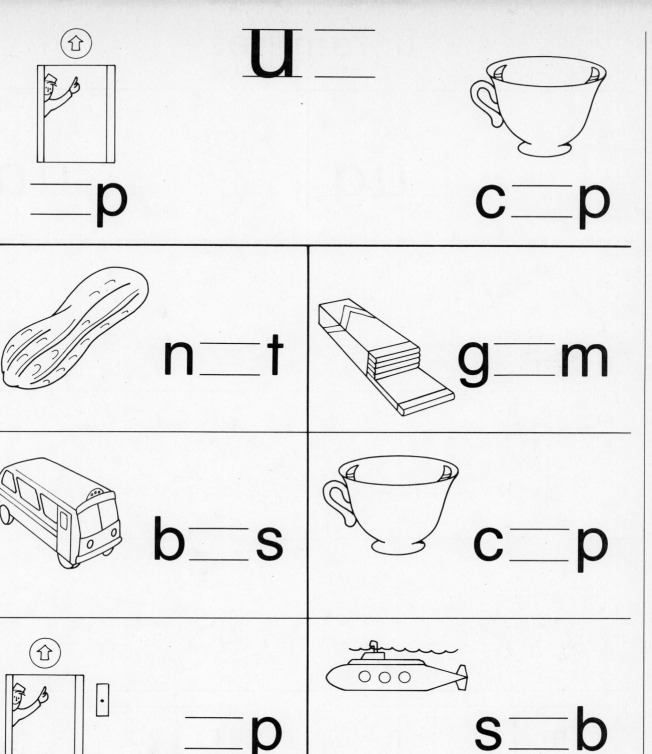

__ __ p

c __ p

n __ t

g __ m

b __ s

c __ p

__ __ p

s __ b

u u u u u u u u

u families

jug   run

u families

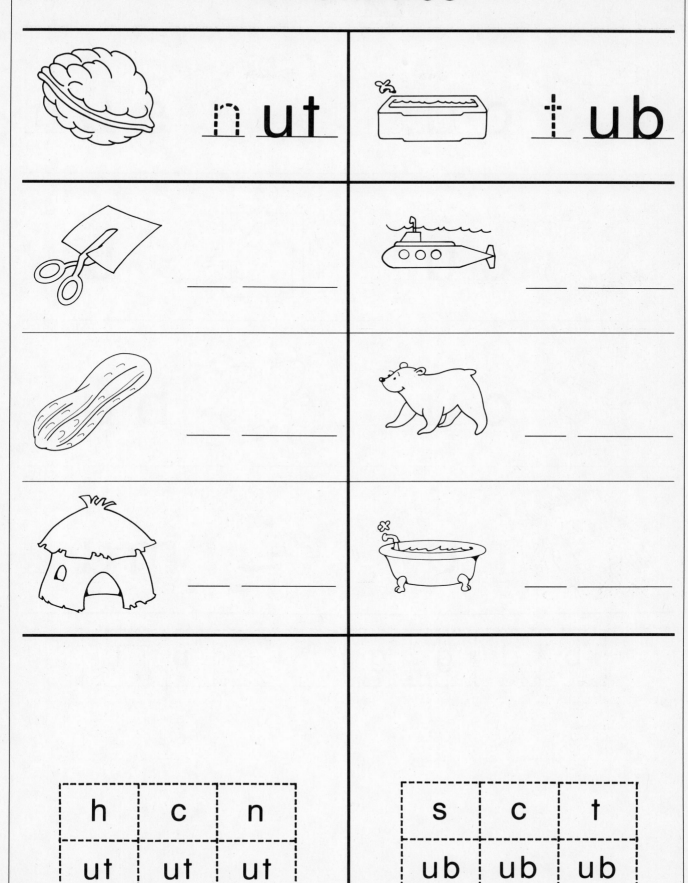

n ut

t ub

h	c	n
ut	ut	ut

s	c	t
ub	ub	ub

u__

 c u __

 s u __

 c u __

 u __

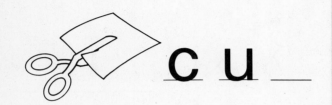 c u __

 b u __

 r u __

 m u __

| b | d | g | g | n | p | p | t |

u _ _

 c u _  m u _

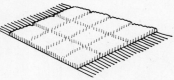 _ u g  _ u g

 _ u _  _ u _

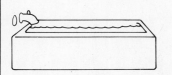 _ u _ 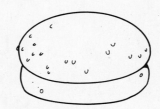 _ u _

 _ u _  _ u _

b	b	b	b	c	g	g	g
h	n	n	p	r	s	t	t

u

b __ s   n __ t   s __ n   t __ b

r __ n   m __ g   g __ m   c __ t

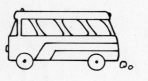
mug

nut
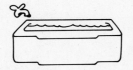

tub

cut
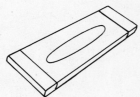

gum

run

sun

bus

---

u

tub	but	tub	tub	tab	tan
pup	pup	pop	pup	pat	cup
sub	but	sun	sub	rub	sub
rug	rug	rug	rag	ran	bug
bus	bat	bus	but	bum	bus

tub

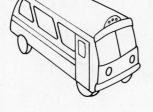

bus

pup

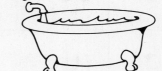

sub

u___

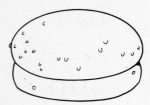

jug

rug

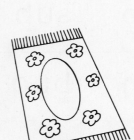

bun

sun

rug	run	rut	rug	nut	rug
bun	bin	bun	dim	bun	pun
sun	sun	son	sum	run	sun
jug	jug	dug	jug	dug	jam
gum	gap	gum	gun	gum	hum

U

  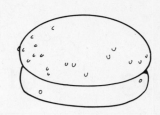 

  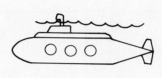

bun	pup	run
tug	jug	cub
cut	up	sub

u __

rug	rut	run	tug	mug	rug
pup	cup	up	bum	bun	bus
bum	bun	bus	bug	tug	hug
tug	hug	mug	gum	gun	yum
hug	jug	tug	sub	cub	rub

U

 The sun is ___ ___ .

 Pup dug up a ___ ___ ___ .

 Mud is on the ___ ___ ___ .

 A bug is on the ___ ___ ___ .

 A pup is in the ___ ___ ___ .

 It is fun to ___ ___ ___ .

| tub | cup | nut | up | rug | run |

Cut the ___ ___ ___.

Bud is in the ___ ___ ___.

The ___ ___ ___ is in the tub.

A bug is on the ___ ___ ___.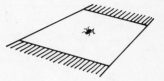

___ ___ ___ the ___ ___ ___.

Pup ___ ___ ___ in the ___ ___ ___.

mud	bug	Hug	dug	pup
bun	rug	bus	sub	tub

I.

_ _ _ _ _ _ _ _ _ _ _ _ _ _ _ _ _ _ _ .

2.

_ _ _ _ _ _ _ _ _ _ _ _ _ _ _ _ _ _ _ .

3.

_ _ _ _ _ _ _ _ _ _ _ _ _ _ _ _ _ _ _ .

I. fun	is	The	pup		
2. in	A	a	bug	cup	is
3. sub	a	A	tub	in	is

| a | | | u 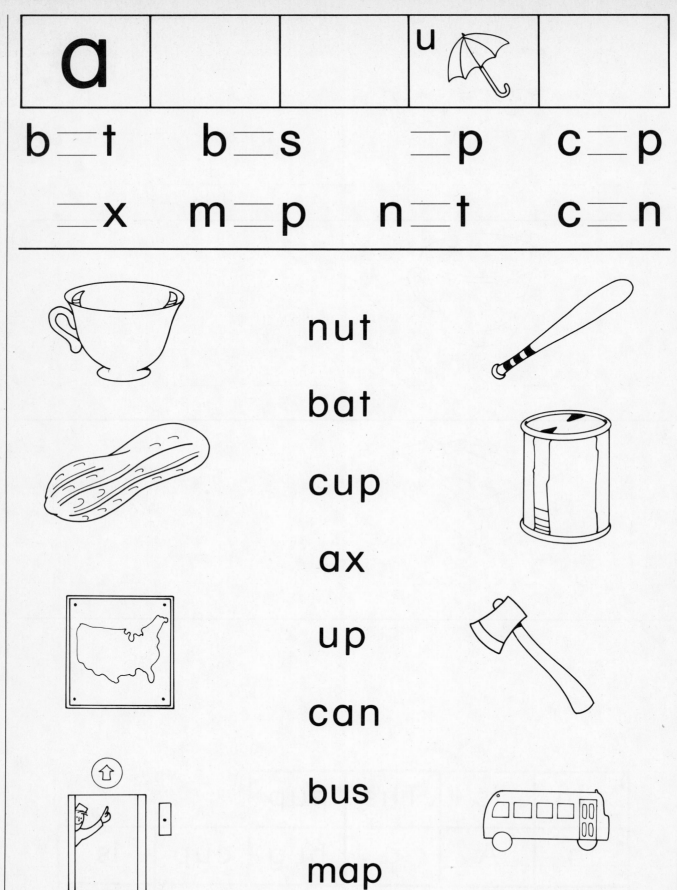 | |

b _ t   b _ s   _ _ p   c _ p

_ _ x   m _ p   n _ t   c _ n

nut

bat

cup

ax

up

can

bus

map

| a | | | u  | |

 b_g

 b_t

 p_n

 f_n

 n_t

 b_n

 r_g

 c_t

 h_t

 c_t

a a a a a u u u u u

| a | | | u | |

cat   can   cut

bag   bat   bug

rat   rut   ran

cut   cup   up

jut   jab   jam

pat   pun   pup

mud   man   mat

gum   gab   gun

sun   sat   sub

can   cut   cat

but   bun   bat

at   ax   an

| **a** | | | u | |

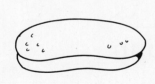

_____

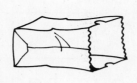

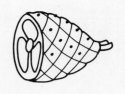

_____

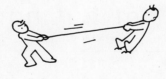

_____

_____

bag	up	fan	sun	ham	bun
rag	hut	tug	bug	mad	sad

| a | | | u | |

1. The can is in the _____.
   bag bug bun

2. The ham is in the _____.
   pan pat ran

3. Jan is in the _____.
   bug bag bus

4. Dad cut the _____.
   hat hut ham

5. Dan has a tan _____.
   hat hum had

6. Pam can nap on the _____.
   ran rug run

7. Dad is a _____.
   mud man mad

	o 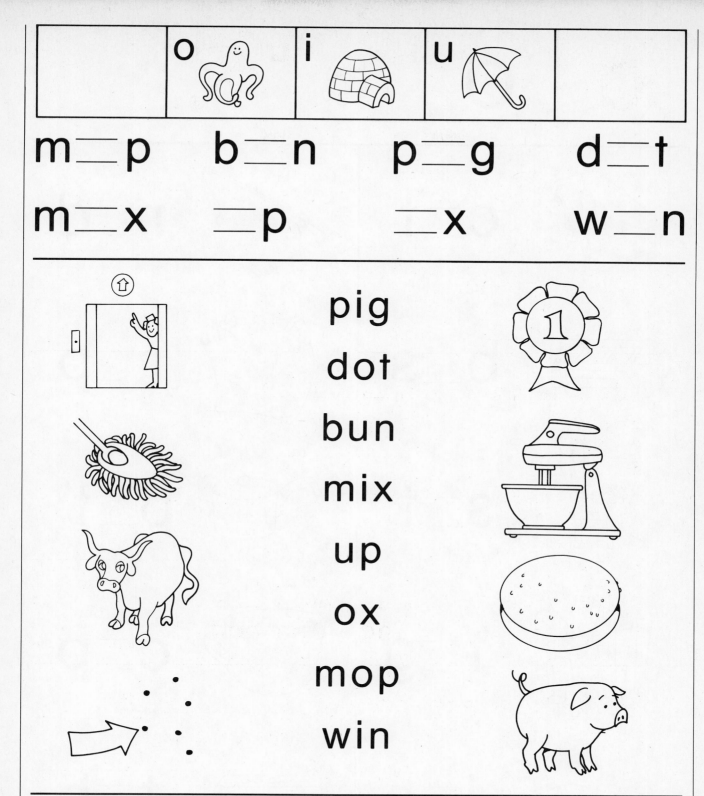	i	u	

m__p   b__n   p__g   d__t

m__x   __p   __x   w__n

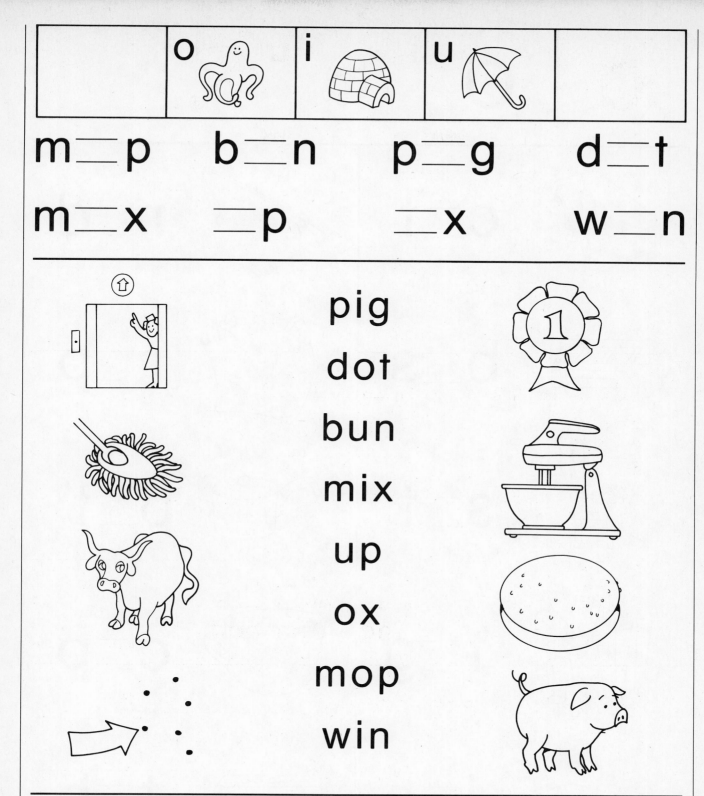

pig

dot

bun

mix

up

ox

mop

win

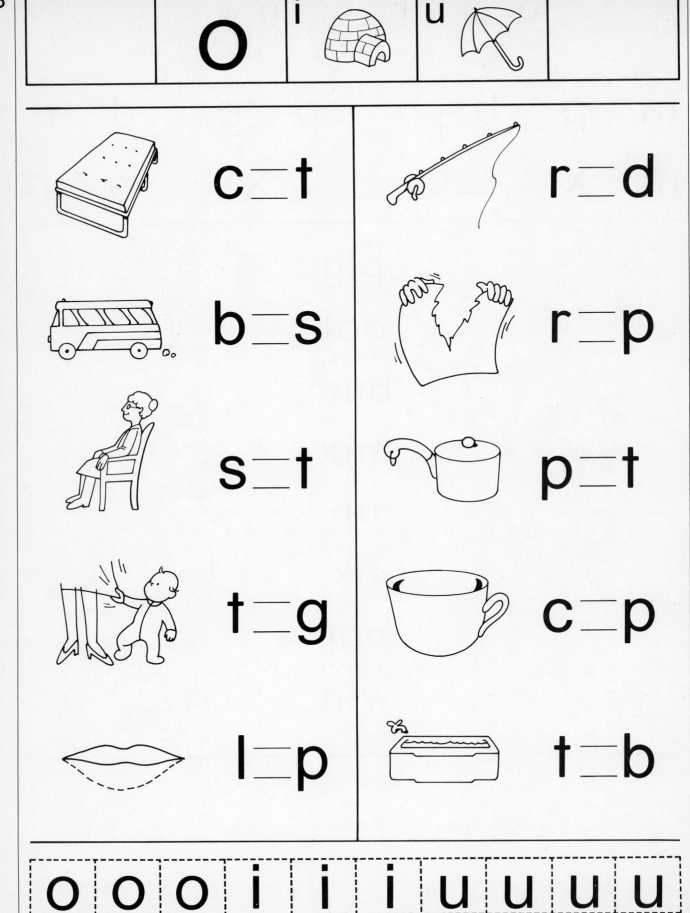

o | i | u

c □ t   r □ d

b □ s   r □ p

s □ t   p □ t

t □ g   c □ p

l □ p   t □ b

o o o o i i i i u u u u

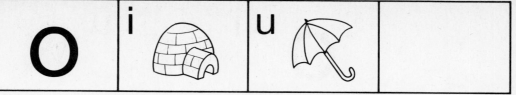

O   i   u

hot hit hut	up on in	dig dug dog
sob sip sub	hit hot hut	cot cut sit
bag bug big	fox fix fun	log big bug
rod wig rug	hot hit hut	rod rug wig

| o | i | 🧊 | u | ☂ | |

| log | hop | hug | pig | sub | sip |
| nut | bib | jog | mix | box | pup |

	O	i	u	

1.

The bug _____ the big cat.

pot bit but

2.

Kim is on the _____.

cap cot cup

3.

Tom had _____ in the sun.

fun fin fan

4.

The bug _____ in the log.

hid hot hut

5.

Mom had a _____ of pop.

sub sap sip

6.

The top did _____ fit the box.

nut not hit

7.

Did the dog run in the _____?

mud mop wig

E＿
e＿

__e__

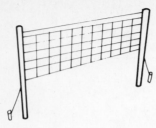

n__t

h__n

p__n

b__d

t__n

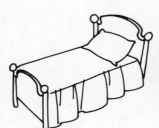

h__n

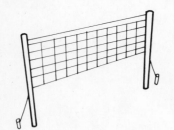

n__t

w__b

e e e e e e e e

e families

 m en    w et

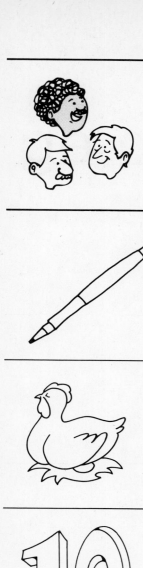 _ _ _    _ _ _

 _ _ _    _ _ _

 _ _ _    _ _ _

p	t	h
en	en	en

n	j	p
et	et	et

e families

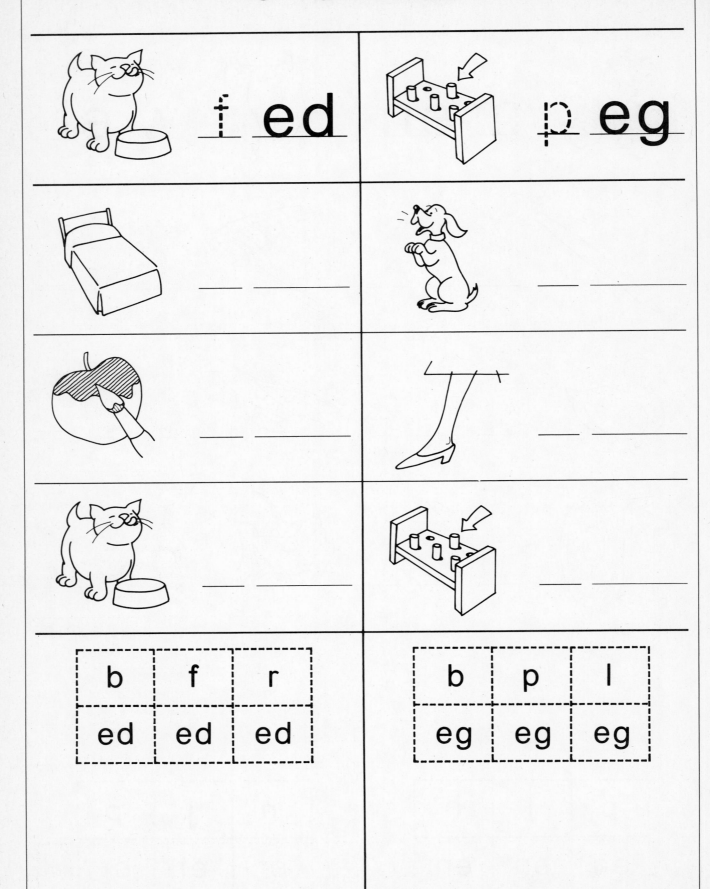

f **ed**

p **eg**

b	f	r
ed	ed	ed

b	p	l
eg	eg	eg

e

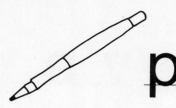 p e _

 s e _

 t e _

 j e _

 r e _

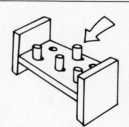 p e _

 n e _

 p e _

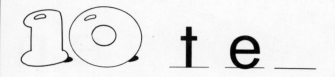

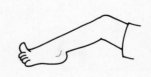 l e _

d	d	g	g	n	n	t	t	t

e _

 p e _    v e _

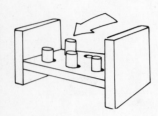 _ e g    _ e n

 _ e _    _ e _

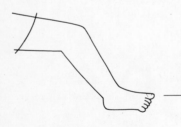 _ e _    _ e _

 _ e _    _ e _

b	b	b	d	g	g	l	m
n	p	p	t	t	t	w	w

e

l__g   w__t   b__g   j__t

n__t   p__t   m__n   t__n

pet

jet

leg

ten

wet

men

beg

net

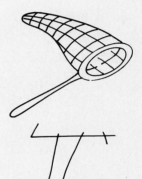

---

e __

hen	ham	hen	pen	hen	ham
leg	beg	tag	leg	log	leg
pen	pen	pan	pen	pin	ban
web	web	wet	met	wed	web
bed	bet	bed	bad	bed	bat

web

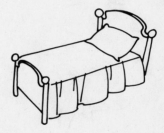

pen

bed

hen

e __

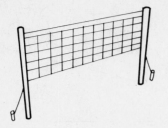

10

ten

leg

jet

net

net	ten	net	not	net	met
leg	leg	peg	beg	leg	beg
ten	pen	ten	tan	ten	hen
jet	pet	get	jet	yet	jet
wet	wed	web	wet	met	wet

e __

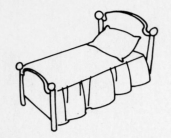 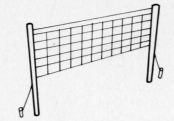 

 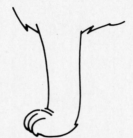 

  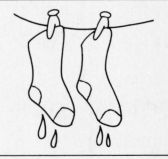

web	hen	beg
net	leg	pet
bed	wet	peg

e __

pep	beg	bed	pen	peg	pet
wet	web	met	ten	pen	hen
met	hen	men	pet	pen	jet
pet	jet	pen	get	peg	pet
wed	wet	red	hen	leg	let

e

 Get the red __ __ __ __ .

 The hen is __ __ __ __ .

   Ted met the __ __ __ __ .

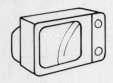 Get the TV __ __ __ __ .

 Ned is __ __ __ __ .

 Ed fed the __ __ __ __ .

| ten | peg | wet | men | set | pet |

Let Jen ___ ___ ___ the hen.

The pet is ___ ___ ___ .

Ned ___ ___ ___ the ___ ___ ___ .

Set the ___ ___ ___ on the bed.

Ben ___ ___ ___ the ___ ___ ___ .

led	pet	net	fed
	men	hen	wet

1.

_ _ _ _ _ _ _ _ .

2.

_ _ _ _ _ _ _ _ .

3.

_ _ _ _ _ _ _ _ .

1. his	Ted	fed	pet
2. met	the	Ken	men
3. red	the	pen	Get

a				e

b_t   b_g   w_b   n_t

r_t   c_p   p_n   t_n

bat

ten

cap

pen

web

net

bag

rat

a				e 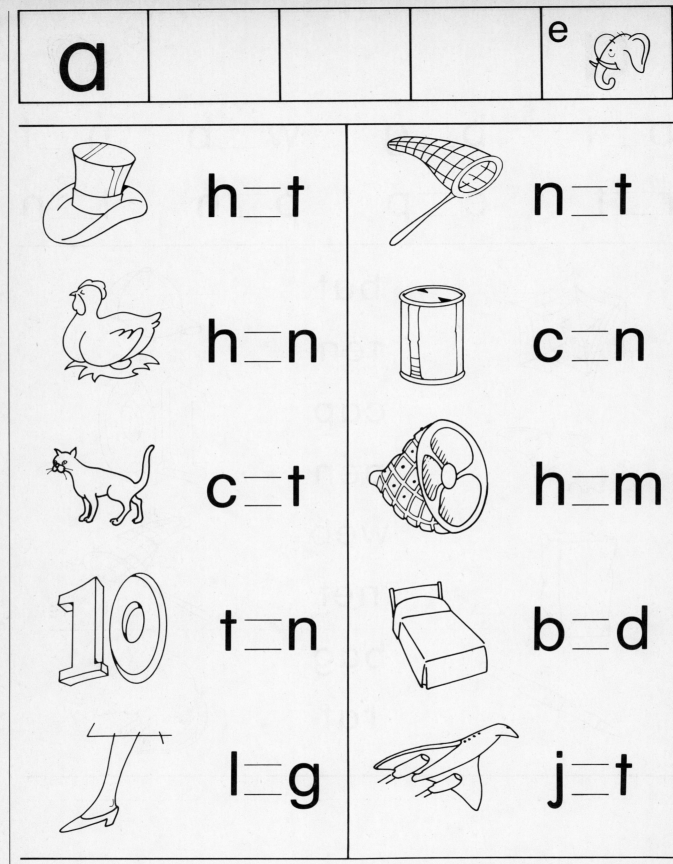

h _ t   n _ t

h _ n   c _ n

c _ t   h _ m

t _ n   b _ d

l _ g   j _ t

a a a a a e e e e e e e

a				e 

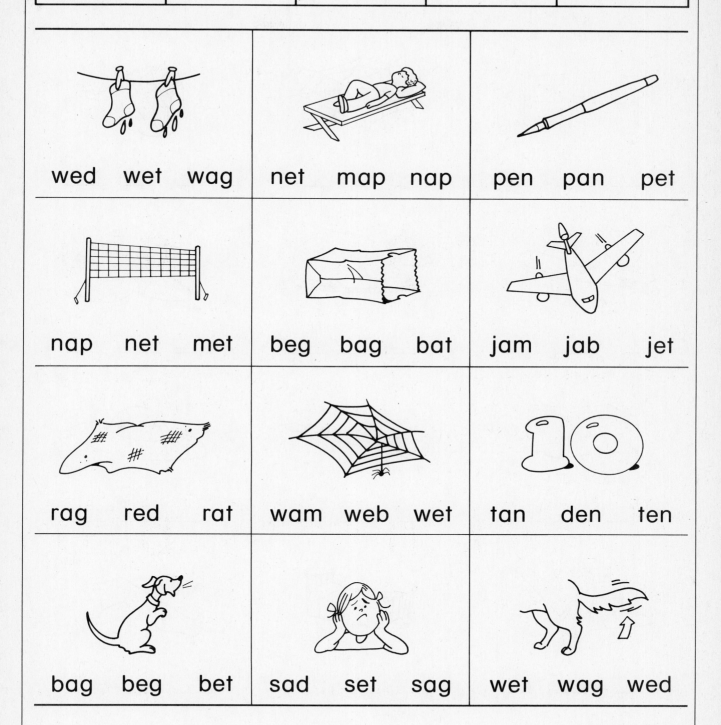

wed   wet   wag

net   map   nap

pen   pan   pet

nap   net   met

beg   bag   bat

jam   jab   jet

rag   red   rat

wam   web   wet

tan   den   ten

bag   beg   bet

sad   set   sag

wet   wag   wed

a				e

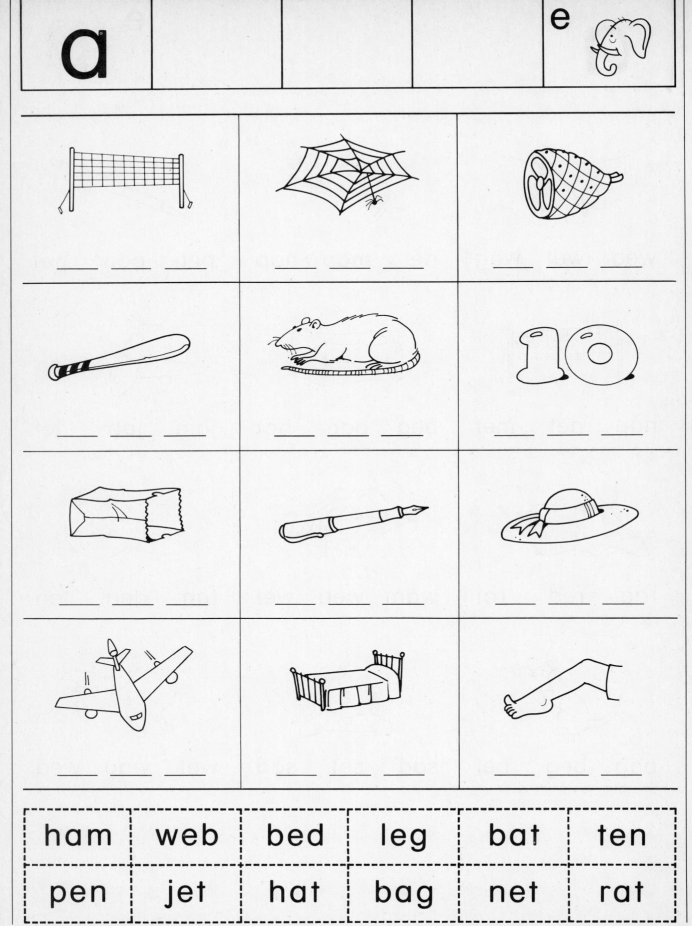

ham	web	bed	leg	bat	ten
pen	jet	hat	bag	net	rat

a				e

1.

1, 2, 3, 4, 5, 6, 7, 8, 9, _____.

tan   ten   den

2.

Ben can sit in his _____.

vet   van   vat

3.

A cat is a _____.

pat   get   pet

4.

Dan can nap in a _____.

bad   bed   fed

5.

The hen can get _____.

web   red   wet

6.

I met a _____.

man   mad   met

7.

Ed has to get a red _____.

pen   ten   pat

		i 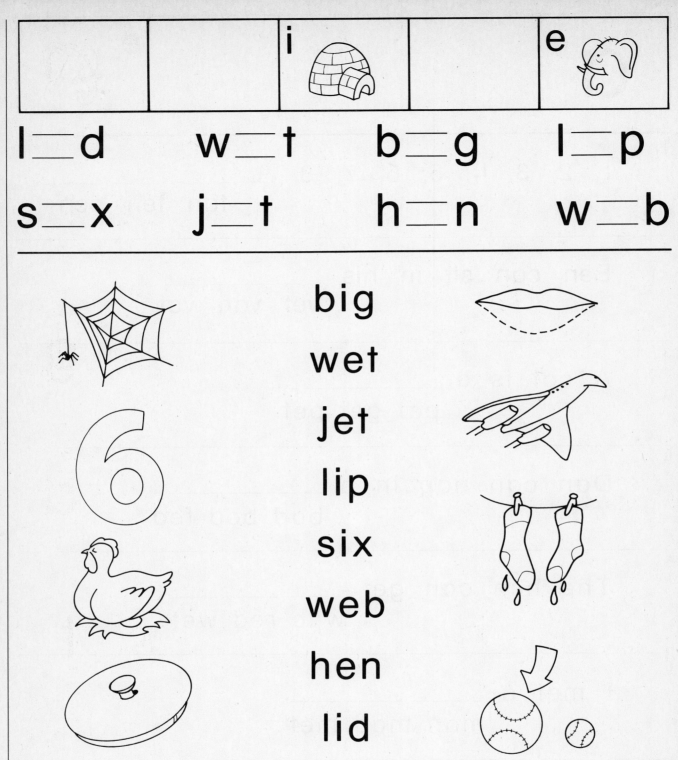		e

l □ d   w □ t   b □ g   l □ p

s □ x   j □ t   h □ n   w □ b

big

wet

jet

lip

six

web

hen

lid

		i		e 

 l_d

 p_n

 t_n

 p_g

 b_b

 b_d

 p_t

 s_t

 h_n

n_t

i i i i i e e e e e

| | | **i** | | **e** 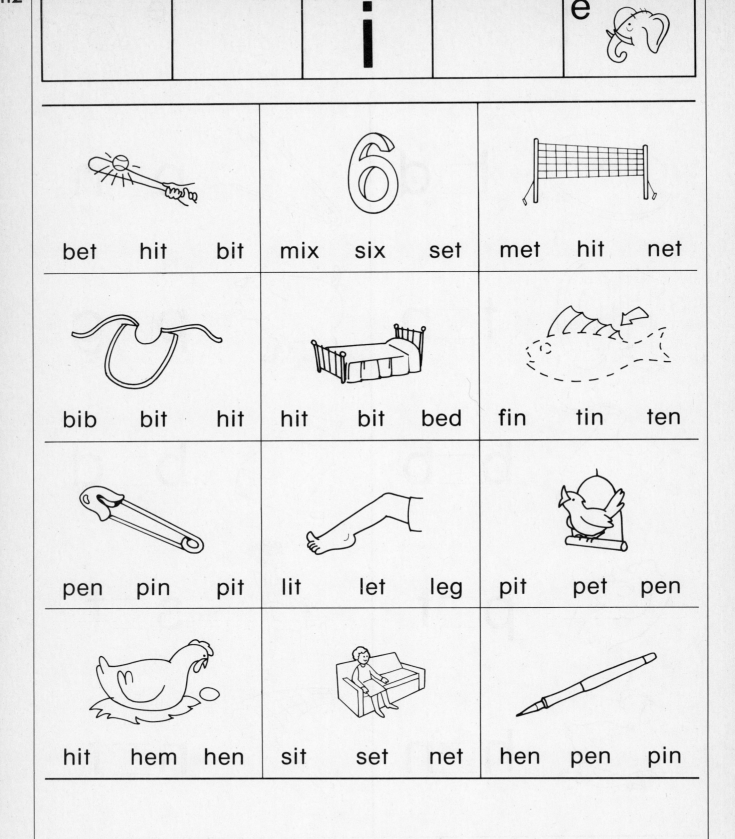 |

bet hit bit	mix six set	met hit net
bib bit hit	hit bit bed	fin tin ten
pen pin pit	lit let leg	pit pet pen
hit hem hen	sit set net	hen pen pin

i	e

___ ___	___ ___	___ ___
___ ___	___ ___	___ ___
___ ___	___ ___	___ ___
___ ___	___ ___	___ ___

ten	dig	zip	pet	pen	fin
leg	lip	wig	jet	sip	web

114

| | | i | | e |

1. 1, 2, 3, 4, 5, _____ .
ten six sit

2. Ted is in _____ .
bit beg bed

3. Jim fed the _____ .
pit peg pig

4. Fix the rip in the _____ .
nap net set

5. 1, 2, 3, 4, 5, 6, 7, 8, 9, _____ .
ten leg tin

6. The pig is in the _____ .
pen pin big

	o		u	e

d☐t   h☐n   t☐g   m☐d

t☐b   s☐t   t☐p   m☐n

hen

tug

mud

men

set

tub

dot

top

	o			u	e

l _ g   p _ t

l _ g   b _ s

h _ t   w _ b

n _ t   p _ p

h _ t   n _ t

o	o	u	u	u	u	e	e	e	e

	o		u	e 

get cut cot	pot pup pen	mug mop met
hen tub ten	sub sob set	beg hog bug
beg hog bug	get cut cot	bed bud pot
leg top tub	hut den dot	cot cup cub

	o		u	e

hug	box	rug	hop	jet	beg
fox	bun	wet	rod	ten	sun

	o		u	e

1. The _____ got wet in the tub.
   pup pep pop

2. Don fed the _____ in the pen.
   bun pet pot

3. The bug is in the _____.
   web run wet

4. Bob pet the _____.
   dug dog den

5. The _____ is on the log.
   rub net not

6. The TV _____ is in the den.
   pet set sub

7. Tom set the _____ in the box.
   on pen pun

a	o	i	u	

l □ g   t □ b   m □ n   d □ t

□ p   p □ g   s □ b   c □ n

dot

sub

man

pig

log

can

up

tub

| a | o | i | u | |

 h_t

 p_p

 f_n

 p_n

 p_n

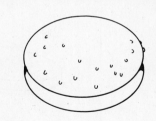 b_n

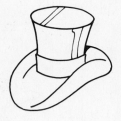 h_t

 p_p

 f_n

 s_x

a a a o i i i u u u

a o i u

bug bag big	lid lad lip	not nut nod
map mop nap	fix fin fox	bug big bag
tub tab bat	bug bag big	map mop nap
map mop nap	wag wig map	tip top tap

a	o	i	u	

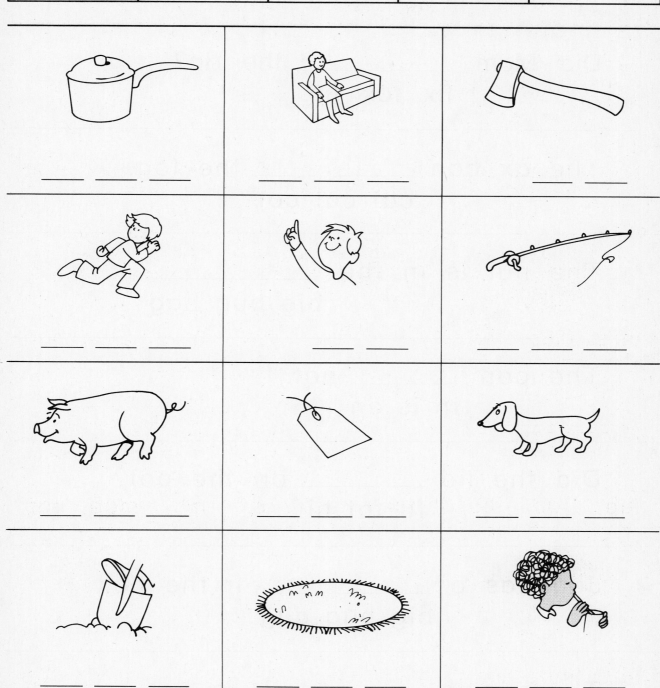

run	sit	pig	rug	pot	up
ax	sip	rod	dog	tag	dig

a	o	i	u

1.

Did Mom _____ the rip?

fix fox fin

2.

The ax can _____ the log.

cat cut cot

3.

The nut is in the _____ .

big bug bag

4.

The pan _____ hot.

in is on

5.

Did the lid _____ on the pot?

fit fat hit

6.

Jim has a _____ in the box.

big bug dug

7.

The sun is _____ . It is hot.

in on up

a	o	i	u	e

_____

_____

_____

_____

_____

_____

_____

_____

_____

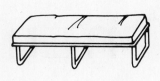

_____

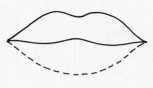

_____

_____

sun	lip	dig	cap	top	wet
cot	fan	cup	web	pin	net

a	o	i	u	e

 m _ d

 s _ b

 s _ n

 _ n

 s _ p

 c _ n

b _ d

 h _ n

a	a	o	i	u	u	e	e

a o i u e

win   men   man   beg   big   bug   leg   log   lag

pit   pet   pot   pen   pin   pan   beg   big   bug

log   leg   lag   pit   pet   pot   win   men   man

pen   pin   pan   beg   big   bug   pen   pin   pan

1. Mom can _____ the pop.

2. A pin can _____ the rip.

3. A bus can get _____ .

4. A _____ can get a map.

5. The lid can _____ on the pan.

6. A cat can _____ in a box.

7. A cap can _____ .

8. A _____ can not get mad.

| fit | rip | rug | fix | gas | man | sit | sip |

1. The dog can _____ .

             big bag beg

2. The _____ is in the pan.

    him ham hum

3. The pig has fun in the _____ .

          mad met mud

4. Six _____ got in the jet.

  man hen men

5. The _____ is on the log.

  big beg bug

6. The _____ has a lid.

  pot pat pit

7. Ben can _____ the rip.

  fox fix tax

1. Can a dog beg? _____

2. Can Mom wax the cat? _____

3. Can a bus get gas? _____

4. Is a top a pet? _____

5. Can a man sit on a log? _____

6. Can a pig sit in the mud? _____

7. Can Tim pet the dog? _____

8. Is the sun hot? _____

9. Can a fox get wet? _____

10. Can a pin hop? _____

| yes | yes | yes | yes | yes | yes | yes | no | no | no |

1. It is big.

   It is hot.

   It is the _____.

2. It can run.

   It can beg.

   I can pet it.

   It is a _____.

3. It is not big.

   It is in the web.

   It is a _____.

4. It is big.

   I can nap on it.

   It is a _____.

5. It is in a can.

   I can sip it.

   It is _____.

6. Mom has it.

   It has a lid.

   It is not a pan.

   It is a _____.

7. It is wet.

   The pig is in it.

   It is _____.

8. I can cut it.

   A hot dog is in it.

   It is a _____.

| dog | bed | bun | sun | mud | pot | bug | pop |

Ben has a _____ _____ _____ cat.

The cat has a _____ _____ _____ on the bed.

Jan _____ _____ _____ a pup.

The pup is on the _____ _____ _____ .

Ben has a can of _____ _____ _____ .

The pup did _____ _____ _____ get the pop.

has	beg	pet	nap
not	rug	pop